D1551025

Trace Numbers and Trace Letters
Workbook For Preschool

SPEEDY
PUBLISHING

Speedy Publishing LLC
40 E. Main St. #1156
Newark, DE 19711
www.speedypublishing.com

Copyright 2015

All Rights reserved. No part of this book may be reproduced or
used in any way or form or by any means whether electronic or
mechanical, this means that you cannot record or photocopy
any material ideas or tips that are provided in this book

Eggplant

SCORE

2/18

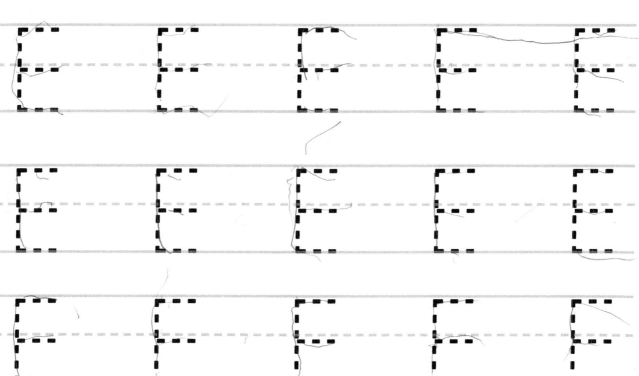

F lower

SCORE

9/18

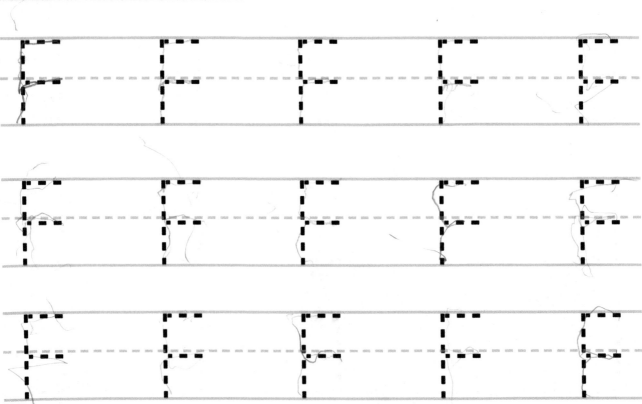

SCORE
15/18

igloo

Jam

SCORE

Kite

SCORE

SCORE

Leaf

Monkey

M M M M

M M M M M M

M M M M M M

M M M M M M

Nelly

N N N N N N

N N N N N N N N N N

N N N N N N N N N N

N N N N N N N N N N

SCORE

Orange

P arsley

SCORE

P   P   P

P   P   P   P   P

P   P   P   P   P

P   P   P   P   P

SCORE

Queen

Rocket

SCORE

R R R

R R R R R

R R R R R

R R R R R

Sun

SCORE

S S S

S S S S S

S S S S S

S S S S S

Tree

SCORE

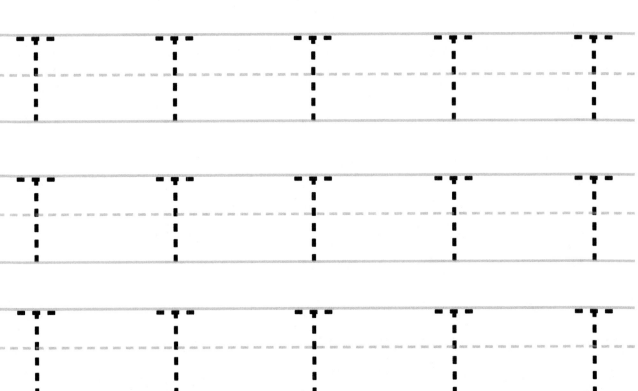

SCORE

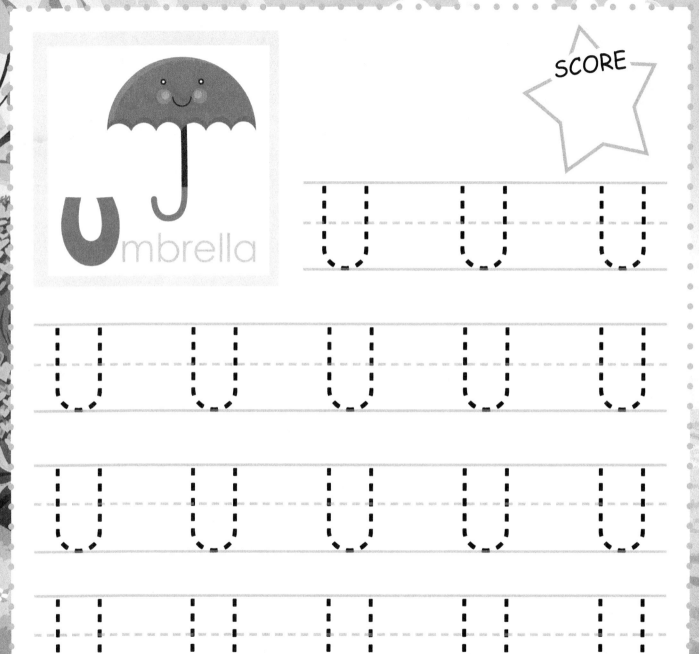

mbrella

Whale

SCORE

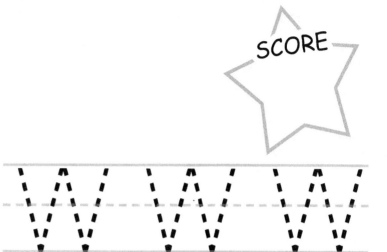

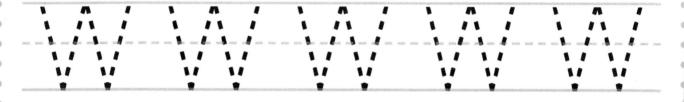

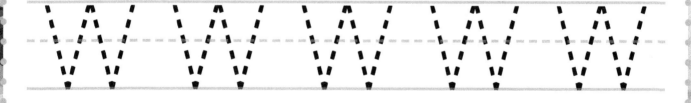

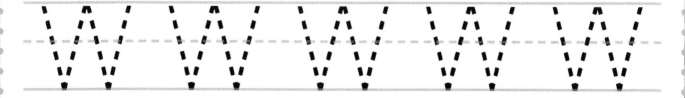

SCORE

X-ray

Y

yo-yo

SCORE

Zebra

SCORE

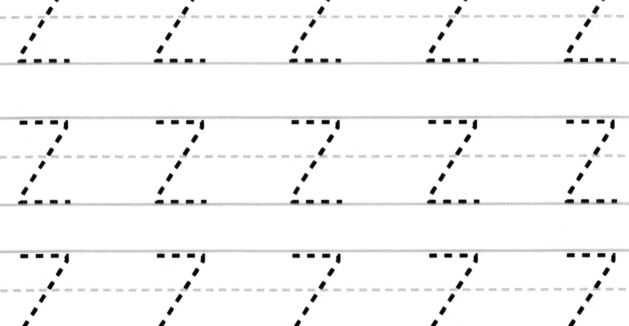

SCORE

a   a   a   a   a

b   b   b   b   b

c   c   c   c   c

d   d   d   d   d

SCORE

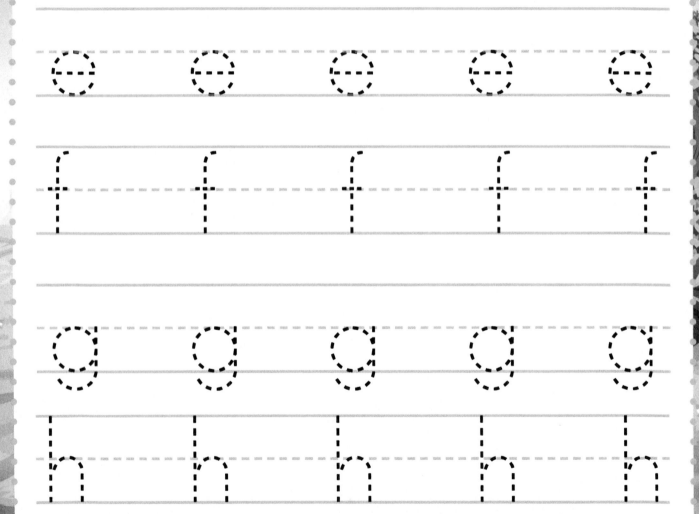

e   e   e   e   e

f   f   f   f   f

g   g   g   g   g

h   h   h   h   h

SCORE

m   m   m   m   m

n   n   n   n   n

o   o   o   o   o

p   p   p   p   p

a   a   a   a   a

r   r   r   r   r

s   s   s   s   s

t   t   t   t   t

SCORE

SCORE

U U U U U

Z Z Z Z Z

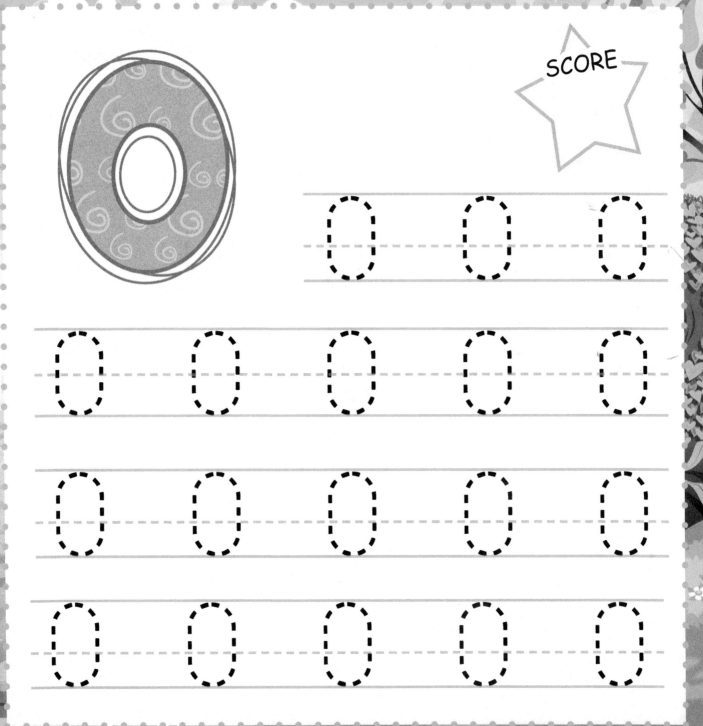

SCORE

Maddon

SCORE

4

SCORE

5

5 5 5

5 5 5 5 5

5 5 5 5 5

5 5 5 5 5

SCORE

SCORE

SCORE

SCORE

CPSIA information can be obtained
at www.ICGtesting.com
Printed in the USA
LVOW02s1934290117
522521LV00009B/177/P